W9-BRD-589

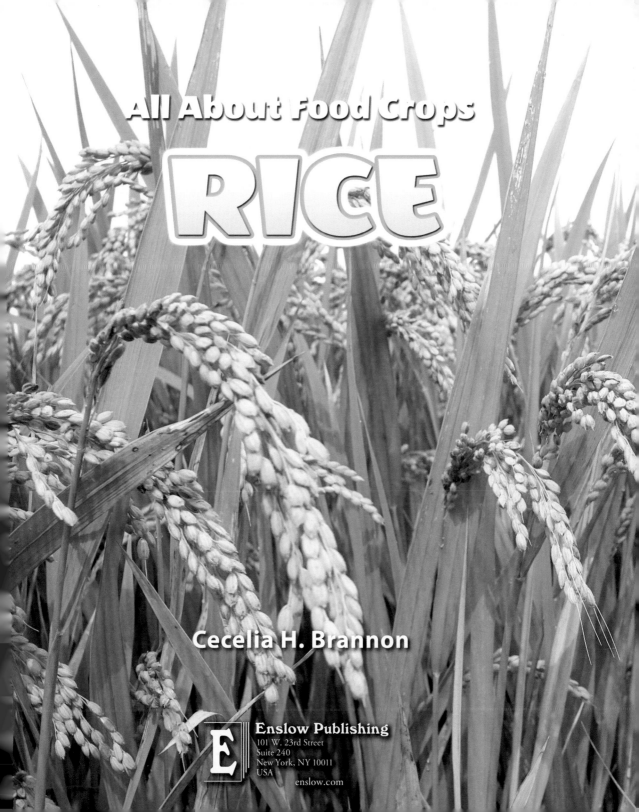

All About Food Crops

RICE

Cecelia H. Brannon

Enslow Publishing
101 W. 23rd Street
Suite 240
New York, NY 10011
USA

enslow.com

Published in 2018 by Enslow Publishing, LLC
101 W. 23rd Street, Suite 240, New York, NY 10011

Library of Congress Cataloging-in-Publication Data

Names: Brannon, Cecelia H., author. | Brannon, Cecelia H. All about food crops.
Title: Rice / Cecelia H. Brannon.
Description: New York, NY : Enslow Publishing, 2018. | Series: All about food crops | Audience: Pre-K
   to grade 1. | Includes bibliographical references and index.
Identifiers: LCCN 2017002024| ISBN 9780766085831 (library-bound) | ISBN 9780766088283 (pbk.) |
   ISBN 9780766088221 (6-pack)
Subjects: LCSH: Rice—Juvenile literature.
Classification: LCC SB191.R5 B675 2018 | DDC 633.1/8—dc23
LC record available at https://lccn.loc.gov/2017002024

Printed in the United States of America

To Our Readers: We have done our best to make sure all websites in this book were active and appropriate when we went to press. However, the author and the publisher have no control over and assume no liability for the material available on those websites or on any websites they may link to. Any comments or suggestions can be sent by email to customerservice@enslow.com.

Photo Credits: Cover, p. 1 zhuda/Shutterstock.com; pp. 3 (left), 6 sotopiko/Shutterstock.com; pp. 3 (center), 16 N8Allen/Shutterstock.com; pp. 3 (right), 12 margouillat photo/Shutterstock.com; pp. 4–5 Tobik/Shutterstock.com; p. 8 Worldpics/Shutterstock.com; p. 10 Africa Studio/Shutterstock.com; p. 14 Iryna Melnyk/Shutterstock.com; p. 18 leungchopan/Shutterstock.com; p. 20 Kathrin Ziegler/Taxi/Getty Images; p. 22 Andi Berger/Shutterstock.com.

Contents

Words to Know 3

Rice 4

Read More 24

Websites 24

Index 24

Words to Know

rice   seeds   sushi
paddies

Rice is an important crop.

4

Rice grows in large, wet fields called rice paddies.

Rice is grown in places where the weather is warm, like Indonesia and India in Asia. Rice is also grown in states like Arkansas and California.

There are more than 40,000 different kinds of rice grown all over the world! Rice can be white, red, brown, or even black!

Rice was first grown in Asia. It is a big part of many Asian foods, like sushi from Japan.

People make drinks from rice, too! Rice milk is popular.

Rice is really a kind of grass, and what we eat are the seeds!

Rice isn't just for eating. It's also used to make paper, rope, and makeup!

It is common to throw uncooked rice at weddings. It is good luck for the couple.

Rice is tasty and good for you, too!

Read More

Rattini, Kristin Baird. *National Geographic Readers: Seed to Plant.* Washington, DC: National Geographic, 2014.

Staniford, Linda. *Where Do Grains Come From?* Portsmouth, NH: Heinemann, 2016.

Websites

Kids Cooking Activities
www.kids-cooking-activities.com/grain-facts.html
Learn more about rice and other grains and check out some tasty rice recipes to try with an adult!

Rice Fest
ricefest.com/all-about-rice/facts-about-rice
Read more facts about rice.

Index

Arkansas, 9
Asia, 9, 13
California, 9
drinks, 15
grass, 17
India, 9
Indonesia, 9
makeup, 19
paper, 19
rice milk, 15
rice paddies, 3, 7
rope, 19
seeds, 3, 17
sushi, 3, 13
weddings, 21

Guided Reading Level: B
The Guided Reading Leveling System is based on the guidelines recommended by Fountas and Pinnell.

Word Count: 144